Olga's Ne

L.L. Owens
Illustrated by Lane Gregory

A Harcourt Achieve Imprint

www.Rigby.com
1-800-531-5015

Mom is reading
in the living room.
Dad and Olga are
in the kitchen.

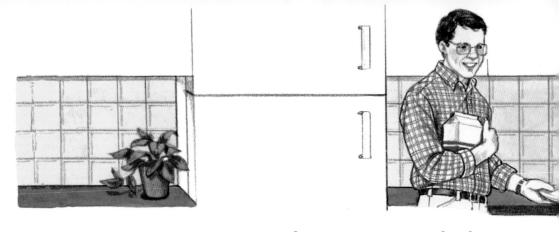

"I want to make a mobile," said Olga.

"Can you get red paper?" asked Dad.

"I can get red paper,"
said Olga.

"Can you get the hanger?"
asked Olga.

"I can get the hanger,"
said Dad.

Olga looks for string.
"The string is not here,"
said Olga.

9

Olga gets tape
from the drawer.

Dad gets rope
from the closet.

"We cannot use tape," said Olga.

"We cannot use rope," said Dad.

"We can use yarn!"
said Olga.

"Mom, please come and
see our mobile!"
said Olga.